CW00448502

SIMPLE
F*CKING
ADVICE
— FOR —
EVERYDAY
HUMANS

-Simeone Crowther Fruke-

Copyright © 2024 by Simeone C Fruke

All rights reserved.

No portion of this book may be reproduced in
any form without written permission from the
publisher or author, except as permitted
by U.S. copyright law.

Simple F*cking
Advice for Everyday Humans
Simeone Crowther Fruke

-Dedication-

In my short time on this spinning rock, I have come to realize many things. First and foremost, that I genuinely know very little. This book is dedicated to all the carbon-based lifeforms that helped me be a little less ignorant along my journey.

Introduction

For those of you who are looking for warm fuzzies and magical unicorn motivation please stop reading now. This is not a book of encouragement and inspiration. It will not pat you on the back, pick you up, dust you off, or hold your hand along life's journey. It is exactly what the title states. Simple Advice For Everyday Humans. If you can set your ego aside and temporarily abstain from being offended you might just learn something about the world and more importantly about yourself. Happy reading and you have been warned.

Chapter 1
SLOW THE FUCK DOWN

We live in a world of instant gratification. Everything is needed right at that moment. We have fast-food orders that always take too long, microwave popcorn that should be done in one minute instead of two, and we have all heard the phrase "a watched pot never boils." That shit is real. The need for everything instantly doesn't just affect the way we approach everyday dining. It bleeds into every aspect of our life.

As human nature goes, we expect this same instant gratification in all physical, mental, and emotional aspects of our lives. We buy our kid that two-hundred-dollar pair of shoes he had to have, and we expect him to automatically put us up for parent of the year. We take that special someone out for a fancy meal and think we automatically have a ticket to shag town. Actual human existence doesn't work like that. If it does, it is a shallow existence, to be sure.

Take a look at the ordinary hamburger. You can fly through a drive-through, snag one off the dollar menu, and instantly enjoy it on your way home. Quick, easy, and it fills your belly with meaty goodness. You could also buy pre-formed patties, season them well, and slap them on your gas grill, which heats up almost instantly. Throw in some fresh veggies and melted cheese, and with a little extra time, you have greatly improved the lowly fast-food burger. Yet if you want to make the experience fantastic, it will take time. From a deep corner of your shed comes the charcoal grill, where you meticulously stack your coal for ignition. You patiently wait for the coals to heat so you can spread them out evenly. Time slowly ticks by as the grill reaches face-melting temperatures, and your burgers can be placed at just the right spot to receive the perfect sear. It is a much longer process, but the reward at the end is far greater than the one you received from the greasy wrapper of the drive-through.

Life is your burger. Your relationships, hopes, dreams, and very existence is your burger. For some things in life, the fast-food version will do just fine, but to get the good stuff, the most valuable parts of your life, you need to slow down. Getting that promotion you have always wanted, winning the heart and desire of that certain someone, and being the person everyone looks up to requires time, reflection, and preparation.

You have to look inside yourself and decide what parts of your life you can be satisfied with at a minimal effort; the McFatty patty at your local drive-through, for example. Then, ask yourself what things in your life are vital. What things in your life are you willing to slow the fuck down for? What things in your life are you willing to give valuable time and effort to? Take some time to make a list. Prioritize what is most important in your life. Put the things essential to you at the top and work your way down. Then decide if you put the most time and effort into those things. If you aren't, don't fucking worry. They won't be on your list for much longer.

The things in our life we make time for and sow into stay in our lives. Those highly valued pieces of our existence require time, patience, and commitment. It doesn't matter if it's your career, relationship, or future dreams and aspirations. We must continuously sow into them to become what we always dreamed they could be. But first, you have to know what the fuck they are.

Slow down, look around you, and, more importantly, look into yourself to identify what has real value in your life. Know without hesitation what aspects of your life: job, people, hobbies, experiences, and even shows to binge you want to carry with you into the future. Once you have done that, your actual journey can begin.

Reflection

If you're always racing to
the next moment, what happens
to the one you're in?

-Nanette Matthews

Guidance

Take a deep breath. Get present in the moment and ask yourself what is important this very second.

-Gregory McKeown

Advice

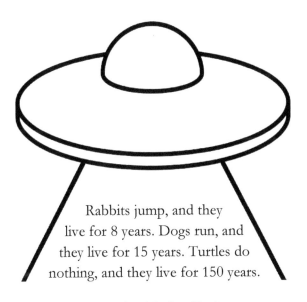

Rabbits jump, and they live for 8 years. Dogs run, and they live for 15 years. Turtles do nothing, and they live for 150 years.

-One Wise Mother Fucker

Chapter 2

SPEED THE FUCK UP

By simply reading the title of chapter two, you are probably already deducing that this book will be rifled with contradictions. What kind of author would advise me to slow the fuck down in chapter one, only to tell me to speed the fuck up in the next? Shouldn't there only be one or the other?

You would be absolutely correct if you were a sea slug living on the ocean floor. You would also be right if you happen to be some vegetative plant life with no real consciousness or genuine ability to take action. Humankind is neither of these things. With complex minds and opposable thumbs, we can tackle problems we face as soon as they arise. Humans have the innate ability to speed the fuck up whenever opportunities present themselves. However, it's our inability to do so that holds us back from so many things. We don't take the bold initiative on a project that could have advanced our career. We fail to respond to the sound investment advice from a friend far wiser in finance. We dive face first into fast food oblivion, knowing it isn't good for us in the long term. Why do we do this? Because it's what we have always done. Often, we find ourselves repeating the same behaviors, with the same intensity, in the same boring jobs, with the same boring relationships, and get by quite contently. Contentment requires little effort. It's boring, and for some, it's a completely acceptable way of getting through life. For others, there is always a yearning for something more.

To further clarify the coexisting ability to slow the fuck down and speed the fuck up, take a look at the fastest land animal on this spinning rock called planet earth. Cheetahs can run more than

70 miles an hour. Some of us never reach that top speed on our daily commute to work, but here is this flesh-and-blood animal, capable of this extraordinary speed.

Ever wonder how often they haul ass into this breathtaking spotted blur? An adult cheetah hunts about once every 4 days. During this hunt, he slows the fuck down and stalks his prey slowly for hours. He observes, analyzes, and takes in his surroundings meticulously. He is mindful of what he is doing, what his prey is doing, and what the world around him is doing. Then, when the moment is perfect, and he sees his opportunity, he strikes. He doesn't hesitate, and for an average of no more than 20- 30 seconds, he speeds the fuck up. Yes, once every 4 days or so, he speeds the fuck up for about a half minute.

As we go through life slowing the fuck down, we have to be just as in tune with our lives as that cheetah stalking his prey. We need to know ourselves, those near us, and our surroundings. We must be mindful of each moment in order to recognize when an opportunity presents itself that we should speed up for.

Maybe it's pursuing a new investment or job opportunity. Perhaps it's about a possible relationship with a certain someone. When opportunities present themselves, we must be bold enough to seize them and ready to speed the fuck up.

Reflection

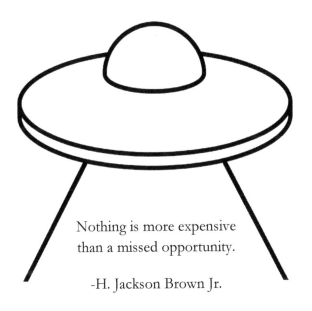

Nothing is more expensive
than a missed opportunity.

-H. Jackson Brown Jr.

Guidance

Life opens up opportunities to
you, and you either take them,
or you stay afraid of taking them.

-Jim Carrey

Advice

Sometimes I want to go back in time and punch myself in the face.

-One Wise Mother Fucker

Chapter 3
FAKE IT UNTIL YOU MAKE IT

There are four levels everyone goes through in their pursuit of being an expert in any particular skill or discipline. Those areas could include business, career, education, relationships, or even enlightenment, but they all progress through these four stages.

Stage 1
You don't know that you don't know.

This is often the most treacherous step. When we start something new, we may think we have it all figured out but fail to grasp how many gaps exist in our knowledge. This results in catastrophic failures as we look for something or someone else to blame but in reality... it's our own damn fault. We see this in the 20-year-old who thinks he can be a day trader based on his YouTube viewing habits. It's also seen in the person who thinks the ability to make a lasagna worthy of Garfield qualifies them to dump their life savings into opening up a restaurant. Sadly, we only ever realize this stage even existed after we have already gone through it. Ever catch yourself saying, "If I had only known," or "If I knew then, what I know now?" Classic examples.

Stage 2
You know what you don't know.

This phase yields tremendous growth as we are more likely to reach out for the advice of others who may have already moved up the rungs of life's ladder. Hopefully, we have swallowed our pride and accepted that we aren't the best at whatever we were trying to accomplish. We recognize that not knowing everything is okay, and the quicker we realize it, the faster we can move on to the next phase.

Stage 3
We don't know that we know.

If all has gone well, if we have slowed the fuck down and sped the fuck up at the right time, we can find ourselves here rather quickly. This is the phase where we sometimes have to "Fake it until we make it." I know the very nature of that statement seems fraudulent. It looks like we lack the ability to accomplish our goals, but it starts with simply taking a chance.

When I first started writing, I had no clue what I was doing, but I definitely pretended to. I wrote a children's fantasy book and leaned on every resource I knew to put it together. Constructed from equal parts Star Wars, Harry Potter, and a dozen other stories and movies, I pretended to be a writer. While the book wasn't a tremendous success, it unlocked further opportunities to present the book, promote it, and learn from the successes and failures of the entire process.

Having this experience where I had to fake it until I made it opened my eyes to what worked well. It also taught me what ultimately proved disastrous, but at least I was learning along the way. What was good and worked I stored away for later; if it didn't work, that knowledge was just as fucking valuable. Life will not always be easy, and mistakes will be made; you can rest assured. Learning from those mistakes as you fake it until you make it can get you to phase four.

Reflection

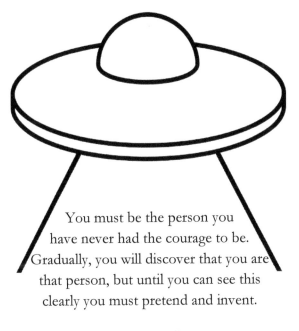

You must be the person you
have never had the courage to be.
Gradually, you will discover that you are
that person, but until you can see this
clearly you must pretend and invent.

-Paulo Coelho

Guidance

To succeed in life, you need
two things: ignorance and
confidence.

-Mark Twain

Advice

All great professionals are
essentially faking it until they make
it. Hence why lawyers practice law,
therapists practice psychology, and
doctors practice medicine.

-One Wise Mother Fucker

Chapter 4

KNOW WHO THE
FUCK YOU ARE

Many people fail along the way in their pursuit of stage four. In this rarely attained stage, you have found confidence. You begin to feel like an indestructible badass in your own element. It's not necessarily arrogance, but you have a swagger about you that is rightfully deserved.

Stage 4
You absolutely know what you know.

It happens when people find their perfect niche, develop themselves within that niche, and understand without any doubt who the fuck they are. Bill Gates was a brilliant inventor. He pioneered radical innovations in the tech industry and revolutionized computer programming and technology. Gates was at the top of his field but put him on a basketball court, and this Harvard drop out wouldn't cut it. Michael Jordan is still the badass of basketball and possibly the greatest that will ever play the game. Put him in front of a computer and tell him to code the software for the latest operating system and watch "Air Jordan" fizzle into the breeze like a stale fart.

Both Gates and Jordan excelled because they knew who the fuck they were. There was no question or doubt. Jordan was dribbling a basketball from the moment he was walking, and Gates worked with code when most of us were learning to write. Gates digitized scheduling programs for his school when he was still a teenager and even hacked it so the schedule would put him in all-girl classes. Who says the jocks always get the chicks?

Yes, both Jordan and Gates are extreme exceptions. They realized who the fuck they were long before most of us even considered what we wanted to be. However, they stuck with it once they knew they were good at something. We all have areas where we naturally excel. When we find our niche, we often give up too quickly because it doesn't give us those instant gratifications we desire. It's easy to see the success of the mega-rich inventors and super athletes and discount it as, "Damn, they got fucking lucky." Take a deeper look at what went into those successes, and you get a much clearer picture.

Look at the bodies broken from wear and tear over years of practice that far exceed our 15 minutes on the elliptical we call a grueling workout. Consider the hours spent with eyeballs glassing over a computer screen, learning and perfecting your use of different coding languages. When considering their complete body of work, we forget that Gates failed miserably at his first startup, and Jordan was cut from his high school basketball team. It didn't always come easy. They just knew who they were and stuck with it.

I am not implying that if you find your groove and stay with it, you will become a billionaire that all admire and adore. I am not saying you will be considered a legend or have adoring fans throwing themselves at your feet. I am saying there is a certain satisfaction in knowing just who the fuck you are.

If you are a school teacher, embrace that and be the best damn school teacher you can be. A writer, write with passion and perseverance, knowing that is what you were made to do. A stay-at-home spouse, make your home an expression of you and what you want your home to be. Bottom line… Embrace the fuck out of what makes you, you! Find what gives you joy and what you are excited to say is an extension of you. Once you do that, whether making millions or making a home, you will have a contentment that no one can take away.

Self-awareness is truly a sign of higher intelligence. If a fish looks at itself in a mirror, it attacks the image it sees. A dog that looks in a mirror often tries to play with the reflection. If a lizard looks into a mirror, it will run and hide from something it doesn't recognize. Young monkeys looking into a mirror will often show mating behavior towards themselves. We are neither fish, forest creature or the pet dog dragging it's ass across the living room carpet. With reflection and determination, we can rise above the lower species and know who the fuck we are!

Reflection

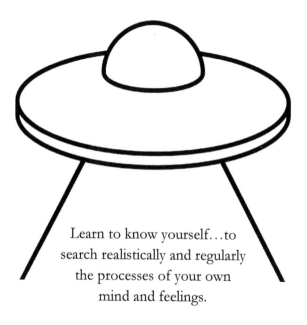

Learn to know yourself...to
search realistically and regularly
the processes of your own
mind and feelings.

-Nelson Mandela

Guidance

Knowing yourself is the
beginning of all wisdom.

-Aristotle

Advice

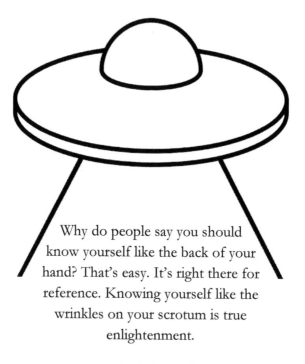

Why do people say you should know yourself like the back of your hand? That's easy. It's right there for reference. Knowing yourself like the wrinkles on your scrotum is true enlightenment.

-One Wise Mother Fucker

Chapter 5

ACT, DON'T REACT

Let me start by saying there will most definitely be times in your life when you need to react. Your ex-spouse swerves at you while walking in the Whole Foods parking lot; you better react. You suddenly realize that your toddler learned to turn on the gas stove and is making his first attempt at mac and cheese... react. You find out that Netflix decided to cancel Stranger Things; you damn sure need to react. In each instance, simple action could have prevented the drastic need for reaction.

Being mindful of where that ex-spouse shops and not being caught open and exposed in the parking lot could have averted your possible experience as a speed bump. Safety measures put on your gas grill and not relenting every time your toddler screams "Mac N Cheese" could have been a solid preemptive move toward mitigating Velveeta mayhem. Looking ahead to find a new show to binge-watch instead of Stranger Things could have… Fuck that! Just cancel Netflix if that happens.

Life is filled with people that are all doing one of two things: They are reacting and responding to the shitstorm life constantly throws at them, or they are acting in a way that helps guide that shitstorm to a place it doesn't affect their daily life, goals, and ambitions. So how do you harness the shit storm instead getting pelted with the downpour like an ant being pissed on by an elephant?

First, realize no matter how perfect or shitty life seems to be going, there is always the potential for it to go in either extreme direction. People will always be looking to push you to either of these extremes. They can't help it. It's their way of keeping the shit storm from hovering over or setting up shop on them. The boss wants to not take the blame for something entirely his fault, so he hard passes the shit storm off on someone else. Then he delights as his unwitting receiver tries to tread brown water in the onslaught of ensuing criticism. Many leap to cast blame whenever they didn't get the job, promotion, career, education, hubby, or wifey they thought they deserved. Yes, even family has been known to sling whatever turmoil they can to make themselves feel better.

It doesn't matter which area of your life we are focusing on. The first step in becoming an actor instead of a reactor is realizing the potential for something to go sideways. It is fucking awesome to be happy and content with your current situation. However, the minute you fail to realize it can change in the blink of an eye is the minute it will.

We have all heard the general concept of Murphy's Law, which states, "Whatever can go wrong, will go wrong." This is one of the most significant mistranslations that has ever existed. It implies that we have no choice. Why should we even try if, no matter what, we will get fucked in the end? The correct phrasing of Murphy's Law is "Things will go wrong in any given situation if you give them a chance."

"If you give them a chance!"

In other words, if you are not constantly looking to act on your situations and are mindful of what you can do to guide the shit storm... you are screwed. This doesn't mean you must constantly respond to everything in your life like one of Pavlov's dogs in a bell factory. However, it does mean you are making sure you are accountable, diligent, and continually proving your worth in your workplace. That way, your umbrella is ready when the boss sends you a shit storm. It means looking over all the things that can impact your most meaningful relationships. Then, when someone tries to damage you, your relationship, or your reputation, you can easily sail your ship away from the ensuing storm.

Learning to act instead of reacting may be hard at first, but it will get easier the more you do it. It will soon be second nature, and you can avoid all the storms Mother Nature, or your boss, may throw in your direction. Until then, lock the gas burner, avoid the ex-spouse and pray to the Netflix gods.

Reflection

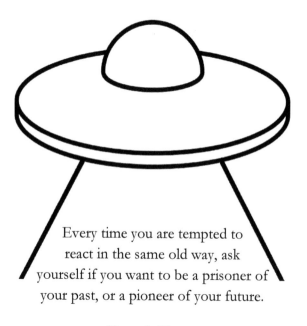

Every time you are tempted to
react in the same old way, ask
yourself if you want to be a prisoner of
your past, or a pioneer of your future.

-Deepak Chopra

Guidance

Consider and then act, don't react.
A worthy opponent will calculate
his move to entice a response from you.
Make your own play.

-R.D. Ronald

Advice

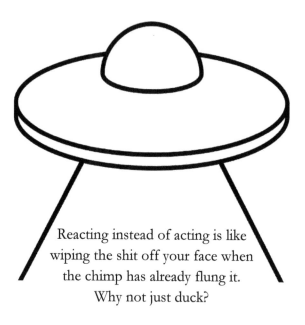

Reacting instead of acting is like
wiping the shit off your face when
the chimp has already flung it.
Why not just duck?

-One Wise Mother Fucker

Chapter 6
DON'T TRY TO FUCKING IMPRESS EVERYONE

We have been transformed into a society that starves for attention. It used to be that humans were nourished by the foods and drinks they put into their bodies, but look around today, and you see people starving for something more. Social media likes and follows have replaced the gastronomical desires of fullness and satisfaction. Most people subsist on a steady diet of Twitter and TikTok, the source of people's fats, proteins, carbs, vitamins, and minerals all rolled into one.

Flip through social media today, and you can quickly get a complete and total rundown of anything and everything your friends and family are doing. What did your best friend from high school wear on their latest vacation? What type of food did your aunt eat at two in the morning? Well, what do you know… sauerkraut and bacon covered with cottage cheese. Best morning breath ever! What's the latest meme, dance trend, fashion trend, food trend, challenge, dare, or hashtag? Don't worry… you will be bombarded by it in good time.

While sharing that much information about yourself with the general public isn't exactly safe, what is expected from that sharing is far more corrosive. We have grown into a society where our self-worth is measured by social media snapshots rather than the rich nuances of actual life. We hold the insignificant likes, dislikes, thumbs-ups, and thumbs-downs above our inward reflection. That outfit only got nineteen likes… into the garbage it goes. No one liked that silly dance I was doing… I'm worthless.

I know that may seem like an extreme and inaccurate description of *you*. After all, it's human nature to want to be accepted and even admired on occasion. Primitive man's ability to establish and maintain social connections is what allowed us to evolve and even thrive in the first place. However, our evolved social nature when taken to the extremes by social media causes two massive fucking problems that warp our perceptions instead of shaping our reality.

First, leaning so heavily on a convoluted display of self and how others present themselves online distorts reality in many ways. I know this may be hard to believe, but not everyone has the perfect family, perfect body, perfect job, perfect dating life, perfect significant other, perfect pet, perfect food, perfect philosophical outlook on life and makes a million dollars in only 4 hours a week. This is seen overwhelmingly in the social media circle, but it's not the truth. Most people on social media are paltry counterfeits of authentic existence. When we buy into the idea that everyone else is perfect, we subconsciously begin to perceive our own circumstances as overly flawed. Often, we see our own life as outright shit.

In reality, families and relationships take work, patience, and the ability to overcome diversity. Jobs most often require hard work and dedication to achieve maximum success. Pets, people, and even philosophy require constant development, shaping, and reshaping to become the pinnacle of what they can be. In other words, it is entirely okay for your life to not be what society would tell you it should be.

More importantly, we must regain the ability to look ourselves in the mirror and say it's okay to be me. It doesn't mean we must be completely content with our job, health, or lifestyle. It does mean we can chart a path for ourselves going forward if we can recognize where we are in the present. We can make achievable goals. Methodically and in our own time, we can shape ourselves into the person we are fully content with, not what society would have us be.

Secondly, when we spend so much energy and effort trying to impress every person on the planet, we dilute the version of ourselves that we give to those most important to us. If that outfit you wore on a date night is on full display for the world to like, dislike, or ignore, was it really something you wore for that perfect someone? Suppose you go around your workplace indiscriminately kissing ass and faking being best buddies with everyone in sight. Would anyone feel like they are genuinely receiving your favor in any way?

Sharing our every intimate detail of life and existence should be reserved for those whose opinions you genuinely care about, not society. Those closest to you will give honest, dependable feedback you can use to shape yourself into a better you. Trying to fucking impress everyone more often has only one actual outcome. You sincerely fucking impress no one! Learn to impress yourself and those whose opinions you sincerely care about. Only then will you find genuine contentment in the life you live.

Reflection

There is only one you. Stop trying to devalue yourself by trying to be a copy of someone else.

-Susie Clevenger

Guidance

Too many people spend money
they haven't earned, to buy things
they don't want, to impress people they
don't like.

-Will Smith

Advice

Don't try so fucking hard to impress others that you lose your own fucking identity. Identify those you hold most dear and be the best fucking you for the people that mean the most.

-One Wise Mother Fucker

Chapter 7

LIFE CAN BE REALLY FUCKING GOOD, BUT IT WILL NEVER BE REALLY FUCKING FAIR

L ife is not fair. Life is really not fair. Life is really, really not fucking fair. Let that sink in. Let it stir up the pain and helplessness those words often inspire. Think about the promotion you didn't get, the clothes you couldn't fit into, the kid that wouldn't listen to you, and the relationship you lost. Think about your relative who has a better car, your neighbor who has a better house, and your friend who seems to have the perfect marriage and home you could only dream of. Think of all the people who seem to have gotten all the breaks in life. Life really isn't fucking fair.

No one could or should disagree with that statement. Everyone from time-to-time gazes into the lives of others and sees those things they often long for. The things that if we could only duplicate in our own petty existence, would make our life that much better. Those with millions of dollars are often striving for better relationships. Those with the most profound connections often cling closely to one another because they lack the material things that can sometimes make life more enjoyable. Hell, I'm pretty damn jealous that Nicolas Cage has a fully intact T-rex skull in his house because I want to be that badass that owns one, but life isn't fucking fair.

When we constantly sulk over the fact that life isn't fair, we dwell on something that serves no positive purpose in improving our lives. It also prevents us from recognizing the underlying reality of our circumstances. Some see a glass as half full and others as half empty. By dwelling on the belief that life isn't fair, we fail to realize that we are in control of the glass itself and the water to fill it up or pour it out as we please. So, let's get it entirely out of the way and all agree.

LIFE ISN'T FUCKING FAIR!

With that now engrained as a basic life fact, we can focus on what is really important. Which part of my life is good, which part isn't quite what I want it to be, and which part am I okay with flushing down the toilet? Start by trying to determine what you are happy with. Instead of saying, "Damn, I could make a lot more money," start with, "I'm happier than a drug dog at a Snoop concert because I have a stable job." Instead of saying, "I wish my spouse and me connected more deeply, "focus on "thank God I've found the person I want to spend the rest of my life with." Instead of saying you will never be good enough, rich enough, or intelligent enough to make it through life, be grateful for your education. Instead of saying you will never find that special someone as you crawl through life in despair, find the things you can grab onto and grow with.

Begin with the things most important to you and focus on improving them. Start with the things you put at the top of your "makes me happy list." If those things are gone, the rest won't be worth nearly as much. Take the things you consider good and focus on making them great. Feed them, water them, and help them flourish in a way you will be proud of. The fruits reaped from this basic little garden will feed you while you tackle the less meaningful shit life throws at you next.

Once your top priorities are set on the proper path, focus on the things that hold a "meh" place in your life. Should you possibly have any of the "meh" things as a higher priority? Are they things you are keeping there out of nostalgia, habit, or just pure stubbornness? If something on the "meh" list should be a higher priority, move it up to the more important list. The list you should spend the majority of your time on. If it isn't, put it on the list of things that deserve less attention.

What you move up will take some time to consistently develop. The stuff you move down consider a part of the third category.

The bottom category is often the trickiest to deal with. Evolution has essentially made mankind hoarders. It made perfect sense for the primitive cave dwellers who didn't know when their next meal was coming. Still, in today's society, it is vestigial. Vestigial is nerdy science talk for something not used anymore but still there. Gallbladders, tailbones, and even your little pinky toes fit in this category; still present but utterly useless. Eliminate those things in your life. Spending energy on things that don't add value to your life takes away from the things that can give you fulfillment and joy. I am not advocating that you never clean your toilet or respond to your boss's memos. However, choose the things that can reverberate back into you the most happiness when given a choice.

Like that, your list of good, meh, and shit items become one streamlined, well-defined area of focus. It won't always be easy. Sometimes even when you focus on improving the good things, there will still be struggles. But at least you will know you are spending your energy on something you genuinely want and need more. Doing so can shift your focus away from the unfairness of the daily and onto how fucking good your present and future can be.

Reflections

Life isn't fair, and it really hurts like hell sometimes. But if you focus on what is within your power to change for the better, you can. And you will.

-Zero Dean

Guidance

Life is not fair, it never was and
it won't ever be. Do not fall into the
trap. The entitlement trap of feeling
like are a victim. You are not.

-Matthew McConaughey

Advice

Life isn't fair. Just ask the dog
when he realizes the cat gets to
poop in the house.

-One Wise Mother Fucker

Chapter 8
NO FUCKING THING SHOULD BE BENEATH YOU

I was taught growing up that nothing is beneath you. However, I was raised at a different time, with a different outlook and different distractions than the world we live in today. I was raised in a small Texas town where things like "hauling hay" and "herding cattle" were a way of life. I was not a cowboy. I was appalled by the idea of wearing boots and never owned a cowboy hat, yet I still had those virtues of hard work and discipline ingrained within me.

I remember the first time I saved up enough money to buy a cow. Yes, the mooing kind and not a reference for computers on wheels, can of worms, or any other catchy acronym. It took every penny I had. Even though my grandpa had hundreds, this one was mine, bought, and paid for. I was beaming from ear to ear when my grandpa asked me, "Looks like you spent every penny you have on it. How are you going to pay to feed it?"

Since hundreds of animals were fed out of the same never-ending surplus of food that seemed never to run dry, I had assumed that is where my lone cow's food would come from. "From the feed room," I sheepishly replied as my smile faded. "That food cost money," my grandpa said, "but we'll make a deal."

Over the next year, my ten-year-old ass would drag out of bed, get dressed, and drive on a barely running three-wheeler to the farm where I fed all the cattle. The entire process took well over an hour. After school, the same damn thing. Raining, sleeting, light, dark, come hell or high water, that was my job to pay for the food of one damn cow. Was that excessive? Probably. Did that teach me a lesson? Hell yes! If a ten-year-old would do that to feed his fucking cow, to what length should we go to feed our fucking family?

I have not always made much money, nor has my wife, but nothing has ever been beneath us. Waiting tables, working at a cabinet shop eighty hours a week, selling on eBay and Amazon, giving plasma, mowing yards, you name it. We have always been willing to do whatever it takes to care for the ones we love. It wasn't always easy or pretty, but the little things mattered. In doing so, we climbed to the top of our careers. We achieved far more than we could have ever achieved otherwise. No shit was ever beneath us.

How did we know how to do this? Because that was the example set for us. I remember my dad owning a dry goods store before the Walmarts and Targets of the world took over. The arrival of these big box stores shut down his and our family's source of income. He owned his own business for years. And now, what was he supposed to do after being his own boss for so long? In the short term... whatever it fucking took. He did manual labor, building fences, cleaning out repo houses, and mowing lawns. Nothing was beneath him until he got a job at the bottom of the pecking order at an appraisal firm. What did he do there? All the little things no one else wanted to do. After the business closed for the day and all assigned tasks were done, he would clean other people's dishes left in the sink. He would go through the office, ensuring everything was perfect before he left. This way, the next day could start more productive than the one before. Was that his job? Hell no! Was it beneath him? Fuck no! Sixteen months later, he was promoted to the boss of those who left a sink full of dishes and the bathroom a mess.

Life will give you nothing. If you sit around waiting for it to do so, you will find yourself living a life of dependence. You will be helplessly tied to a society and system that determines your prosperity, content with the scraps it leaves for you. It isn't always fun and rarely easy, but the big things get far more attainable when you start taking on the little things. When you realize that nothing should ever be beneath you, you also choose to depend upon the person you should be able to count on the most; yourself. This allows you to chart your path forward, advancing under the power of your own two legs, and putting your future into your own two hands. In that, you find absolute freedom.

Reflection

Doing the little things well
is a step towards doing the
big things better.

-Vincent Van Gogh

Guidance

It's the little things that
are vital. Little things make
the big things happen.

-John Wooden

Advice

If all the little things are
beneath you, I can assure you the
big things will always be out of your
reach. We build our ladder out of all
the little things to reach the big things
that our heart desires.

-One Wise Mother Fucker

Chapter 9

YOU CAN'T ALWAYS GET WHAT YOU WANT, BUT HOPEFULLY, YOU CAN FIND OUT WHAT YOU REALLY FUCKING NEED

Humankind developed with a very distinct drive to always want more. It is in our pre-determined genetic makeup. History has proven this fact time and time again. From the conquering of nations to the influence of media, it is part of our very existence to always want more: more attention, more power, and more influence.

We live every day in a world of want. Do we really need that dress, or do we want it? Will we die without that last trip through the drive-through, or does it simply break the monotony of the boring drive home from work? Did we need to binge-watch every episode of Game of Thrones over the 3-day weekend, or was it simply something we wanted to do?

Want and need are often a matter of perspective. I know that may be an oversimplification, but look at it regarding the three absolutes for existence. We can all agree that we need food, water, and air. Without these, you will meet the same fate as those who crossed Tony Soprano and were gifted new concrete boots. I would argue, however, that even these rudimentary things can be categorized as wants, not needs.

Humans can live for three months without food, three days without water, and three minutes without air. I would argue that someone without food and water for three days needs water and probably only wants food. Likewise, someone who hasn't had oxygen for two minutes couldn't give a rat's ass about a soda or something to eat. It just comes down to perspective.

When we shift back to a more realistic view of our lives, we can characterize millions of things we want. Without those, we are left with only a few high-priority things we need. I am in no way saying you shouldn't have and also enjoy the wants in your life, but we need to keep them in perspective. Our insatiable pursuit of wants should never get in the way of obtaining our needs.

Wants are important, though. One of my favorite snacks is popcorn, especially when watching shows. Popcorn nourishes me and pushes me through the extended weekend binge-watching of Game of Thrones. I need the popcorn to give my cells energy, which does the trick. Popcorn alone could do this quite quickly, but I want butter and salt. Without the butter and salt, the popcorn is much less enjoyable.

Using the needs to help us obtain our wants in life is essential. Just make sure the wants really do help push you to the needs. All of us have been guilty of getting this confused in the moment. How many pieces of amazing workout equipment have you purchased that turned into clothes racks? Me too. I thought the want would help me get to the need but ended up wasting money on something I was only interested in for a month or two.

Wants can be positive influences within us when used correctly. Want to slim down two jean sizes but need to lower your blood pressure? That's a prime example of wants driving needs at its finest. Want to make more money so you can afford those season tickets but need to get that promotion or raise for your family's financial security? Bingo, you did it again.

The priority placed on our wants versus our needs is just as important as the timing. I have to admit that I have a tendency to be the ultimate procrastinator. This was never more evident than when I was working through college and had a big exam on a Monday. I was in college, for God's sake. What were weekends supposed to be for? Knowing I still had that big test, I often used Friday to relax with friends and enjoy life. Saturday meant sleeping until noon, then having a little downtime, party time, or just "me" time. When Sunday evening rolled around, I was miserable as I inevitably pulled an all-nighter stressing over the test to come.

The insane thing about putting off your needs to enjoy your wants is that the needs are never really put off. Hanging out on Friday, the worry of that test coming up was always there. It took away from how much I could enjoy the wants of the moment. The same thing happened again on Saturday, as I continued to worry about the test to come. If I had only gotten the need out of the way first, I could have completely enjoyed the wants of my weekend.

This is true for all of us. No matter how much we don't want to think about the needs, they will always be there. It is our job to give them priority and take care of them first. If we do that, we can fully enjoy the hell out of the wants that give our life the flavor and spice that make it worth living.

Reflection

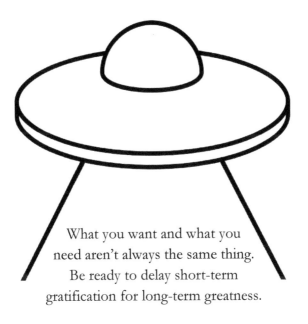

What you want and what you
need aren't always the same thing.
Be ready to delay short-term
gratification for long-term greatness.

-Mandy Hale

Guidance

You have to do what you have
to do before you can do what you
want to do. It's called priorities.

-Oprah Winfrey

Advice

It's a wise fucking person who realizes that they want too many things and, above all, needs to want less.

-One Wise Mother Fucker

Chapter 10

KNOW WHAT YOU KNOW AND WHAT YOU FUCKING DON'T KNOW

I like to think that I am an expert on many things. The stark reality is I am an expert on many things while talking about them, and not so much once I start doing them. Take, for example, my beautiful 2000 Camaro. I loved that car and took great pride in caring for it. I changed the oil, spark plugs, filters, and even brake pads. When the fuel pump went bad, that was another story.

After calling the local auto repair shop, I was quoted a price of $1200 to replace the pump that had gone bad. A quick Google search and I realized this was absolute highway robbery. The part itself was only $220. Could it really be that hard? I set aside a Saturday and went to work as the sun rose.

Contrary to what I initially believed, changing the fuel pump in my Camaro was unlike changing the oil filter. First, you had to get to the damn thing, which required removing my exhaust system. With bolts completely seized with rust, pulling it was near impossible. Then I had to remove the gas tank to access the fuel pump. After hours of work, I gave up and called in a repairman the following Monday.

I talked a pretty badass game to my wife and kids. Anybody could do this job. How hard could it be? I quickly realized I was not an expert and would have saved hours if I had just accepted what I didn't know. Much worse, I had to eat my words embarrassingly for not realizing it sooner.

Knowing what you don't know is just as important as knowing what you do know. When we recognize what we aren't experts on, it gives us a path toward growth and development.

Identifying the areas where we can grow can lead to our overall improvement. No one will be an expert in everything, but we have all been around someone who thought they were. How did you perceive that individual? A blowhard? Arrogant? Ignorant? Probably all three, and justifiably so.

It's not enough to recognize our growth areas, and just acknowledge that we are not experts in everything. We must also be willing to grow in those areas in which we are lacking. The easiest way to do so is to yoke up with those who actually are experts.

I didn't know how to change the fuel pump in my car before, but I certainly do now. Why? Because I sat out there every hour of the procedure watching, observing, and asking questions. Was this probably a bit annoying to the mechanic? Yes. Will I have to pay $1200 ever again if it goes out? Hell no!

Babies have this shit down. What is a baby an expert at? Absolutely fucking nothing unless shitting on themselves is a worthwhile skill to master. So, they watch, learn, and mimic their way to learning things we take for granted. Talking, walking, and all non-verbal communication are learned because, as babies, they don't know shit about being human. They pay attention to those who are better at it than they are. They haven't developed an ego that thinks it knows everything and, therefore, much more quickly absorbs the world around them.

There is absolutely nothing wrong with not knowing something. There *is*, however, something wrong with not recognizing it. Recognize what you don't know just as much as the shit you do. With that knowledge, you are ensuring your growth going forward.

Reflection

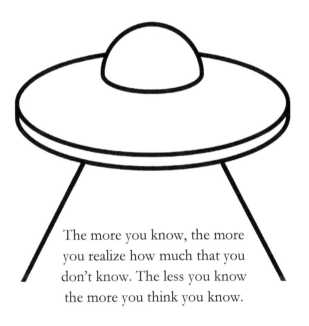

The more you know, the more
you realize how much that you
don't know. The less you know
the more you think you know.

-David T Freeman

Guidance

It ain't what you don't know that
gets you in trouble. It's what
you know for sure that just ain't so.

-Mark Twain

Advice

A person knows that he can
skydive without a parachute, and he
is correct. What he doesn't know…
that he wished he knew…
is he can only do it once.

-One Wise Mother Fucker

Chapter 11

YOUR WAY IS NOT THE
ONLY FUCKING WAY

Reading books as a kid was one of my favorite things to do. It was easy for a young imagination to be swept away to magical worlds, the wild west, or deep space by just turning pages. My favorite books, however, were the choose-your-own-adventure kind. Remember those?

The ones where you are sweating your ass off running from the swamp ghoul when you come to a critical decision. Do you choose to take the ladder down into the basement and turn to page 54 or run outside the house and turn to page 97?

I decided to run outside, of course, where I tripped going down the stairs spraining my ankle and was quickly absorbed by the swamp ghoul's slimy tentacles.

No worries. I just turned back a few pages and chose the other path down into the cellar, where I discovered the wand of light and quickly turned the swamp ghoul into a bubbling mess. Game over; I win.

What I loved about those choose-your-own-adventure books was that there was always another way. You were given options, just like you are in life, and thus the opportunity to choose your path going forward. Unlike in real life, you had unlimited do-overs to ensure you got it right.

When I was in high school, I was really good at math. Today, a twelve-year-old would calculate circles around me, but I was pretty damn good back then. I could even do most of the work from my Algebra class in my head without showing the necessary steps. This frustrated my teacher Mr. Applegate so severely that he decided to make an example of me one day.

"Kid… go to the board," he told me. "Winston, you go too."

Winston, as you may have already guessed, was damn smart. In fact, he graduated high school in his sophomore year to go to college on a full math scholarship. On this day, however, he was supposed to make an example out of me.

Mr. Applegate quickly gave us a math problem to solve, and as the last bit of the problem exited his mouth, Winston's chalk dust began to fly. I looked at the problem, wrote a couple numbers, and erased it. Then I wrote the correct answer on the board and circled it as I began to feel the heat from Winston's furious chalk strokes making the way to my side of the board. A minute later, Winston finished, dramatically dropping the chalk, stepping aside to reveal we'd arrived at the exact same conclusion.

The class giggled as Mr. Applegate began explaining how easy the problem was and that things were not always so simple in life. He gave us another problem longer than Harry Potter book five, and Winston chalked into action.

I looked at the puzzle, wrote a few things down, erased them, and scribbled a bit more before turning around and leaning against the board.

"This is stupid," I lamented. "No one would ever have to solve a problem like this in real life."

Over the next five minutes, which seemed more like five hours, the ranting continued. Mr. Applegate lectured me in front of the class about how those taking shortcuts would end up drug addicts in gutters and amount to absolutely nothing in life. At one point, he even started making up a song about not taking the easy way. I wish I could remember the lyrics because I'm sure it would be a top billboard hit. As a cloud of chalk dust settled over the entire class, Winston came to his solution and circled it on the board.

With a smile from ear to ear, Mr. Applegate exclaimed, "And that kid is why there are no shortcuts in life!"

As I slowly peeled myself away from the board, I responded, "Well, I guess I'm just an idiot then."

The class began to giggle slowly until it burst into a full roar of laughter. Mr. Applegate's face turn red. "Go to the office now," he told me.

Behind me, on the board where I had been leaning, was the correct answer to the problem I had solved several minutes earlier. It was there when I was being belittled and lectured and there while Winston blazed away with the step-by-step approach.

Surprisingly, I didn't get in trouble in the office. It's hard to get a student in trouble for getting an answer correct, even more so when he does it faster than a guy named Winston.

What Mr. Applegate failed to realize is that just because things have always been done that way, it doesn't mean there aren't other ways; or better ways. As evolving humans, we must constantly evaluate if the same approaches we have traditionally used are still effective. If they aren't, we have to be willing to adapt and change.

Those who fail to see other ways of thinking and doing are the ones that get left behind. If they never evolve their mindset, they even run the risk of becoming obsolete. Open your fucking mind and realize that conventional wisdom may not be as effective as it used to be. Your way is not the only way. If life teaches us anything, it's that there are infinite ways to solve life's infinite problems. Embrace life's diversity in thought and action, for it is the key to unlocking untapped potential and navigating the ever-changing landscapes of our world.

Reflections

You have your way. I have my way. As for the right way, the correct way, and the only way, it does not exist.

-Friedrich Nietzsche

Guidance

If you continue to think the way
you have always thought, you'll
continue to get what you've always got.

-Kevin Trudeau

Advice

If only one way is the right
way, why does Baskin Robbins
have 31 fucking flavors of ice cream?

-One Wise Mother Fucker

Chapter 12

DON'T MAKE BIG DECISIONS WHEN YOU ARE REALLY FUCKING HAPPY OR REALLY FUCKING MAD

We could also easily add here to not make big fucking decisions when you are really sad, confused, annoyed, or even horny. Bottom line, don't make big decisions when you are not emotionally stable. For some of us, that may be easier said than done. Sometimes it's impossible to make absolutely clear-headed decisions, but we should at the very least strive for it. Even if that means stepping back and taking a breath before making our next move forward.

I was reading a health article on getting in shape a while back. If you are like me, you look over these from time to time with the greatest of intentions. Everyone is always looking for the next magical trick or shortcut to completely erase the need for a sensible diet and consistent exercise. The advice given in the article really made an impression.

While most articles sell their idea as being as simple as taking a magic pill, or as difficult as 2-hour workouts 27 times a week, this suggested something unorthodox. It advised you to stuff yourself with a mega meal. It didn't have to be a good one, either. Burgers- go for it. Unlimited taco Tuesday- knock yourself out. All you can eat baby back rib buffet-eat just short of a food coma. Nothing and I mean nothing, was off limits. The key was when you could eat that meal.

While you may think it would be early in the day or some magic cheat meal, it wasn't. The key was to stuff yourself before shopping for that week's groceries. The idea was that you would naturally steer your food choice to lighter options when you were already uncomfortably full. Who feels like deep-fried taquitos when you could vomit any moment from overstuffing yourself on taco Tuesday. Surprisingly, it worked. The hungry shoppers bought 60% more calories of food than the shoppers who had stuffed themselves.

This same application can be applied to our own decision-making. We, as humans, are naturally volatile creatures. No, I'm not saying you find the need to "Hulk Smash" every time something doesn't go your way, but even the most reserved of people are greatly influenced by emotions. Why do you think there are so many philosophies and religions set to squelch this very thing from happening?

Emotions make us human, and I firmly believe we must embrace and listen to them. They help guide us down this pathway of life. We, however, should be leading them as we stumble along and not the other way around. It's perfectly okay to stir your emotions. You may even need time to calm, cheer, or control yourself, but this is not the time to make big decisions.

Did your boss pile an extra shift or a ton of work on you? Probably not the best time to sit down and tell him what you think about office management. Did that certain someone tell you how magical your date this weekend is going to be? For God's sake, stay off the shopping websites!

Our natural checks and balances tend to run low when our emotions run high. Again, it's perfectly okay to be pissed at something or someone. It's also great to be excited about the upcoming date, but let those extreme emotional explosions pass before making any big decisions. The big decisions are best made in the Goldilocks zone. The one that's not too hot and not too cold but just right. This is where we can embrace this little concept of logic and level-headedness. It's also where we can keep from feeling like a total ass a few days later.

Reflections

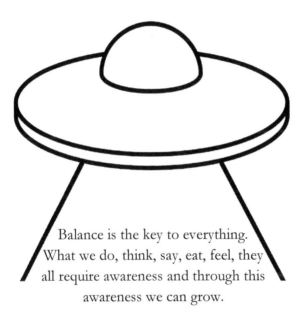

Balance is the key to everything.
What we do, think, say, eat, feel, they
all require awareness and through this
awareness we can grow.

-Koi Fresco

Guidance

Balance every thought with its
opposition. Because the marriage
of them is the destruction of illusion.

-Aleister Crowley

Advice

Life is all about balance.
Remember, money doesn't buy
happiness, but it's often way more
comfortable to cry in a Ferrari.

-One Wise Mother Fucker

Chapter 13

TURN STUMBLING BLOCKS
INTO STEPPING STONES

It has often been said that there are only two sure things in life: death and taxes. I would say there are actually three: death, taxes, and that everyone at one point or another fucks something up. It doesn't matter how careful you try to be or how meticulous you are in every facet of your life. You are inevitably going to mess up.

That's okay. Show me a person who has gone through life never fucking up, and you are showing me a person who has never lived. Fucking up is a normal part of life and is needed for us all to grow and evolve. How you respond when you fuck up, though, is the key to your own development or lack thereof. In my experience, there are five specific ways people respond when fucking up along life's journey.

First, there is the blamer. You know the type. No matter how big or small the fuck up, the blamer refuses to admit they had any part of it, or that it was something out of their control. They seek out anyone or anything they can find to make sure no responsibility falls in their lap. "It was the other driver," "the boss said to," and "I'm sorry they didn't understand" are common phrases tumbling from their lips. It is often far easier to project responsibility elsewhere than to take it ourselves. I have been guilty of this on more than one occasion, and so have you. It's okay to admit it.

The second relatively easy trap to fall into whenever adversity arises is one I refer to as the "Eeyore" approach. Yes, that lovable jackass from Winnie the Pooh who laments about the dire nature of everything.

What? You fell down and stumped your toe?

"I guess that's all toes are really good for."

Wait a sec. You skinned your knee when falling, and it might get infected.

"I guess bacteria need a place to live too."

Eeyore mentality refuses to admit they have any control whatsoever. Life sucks, and simply ignoring the fact it sucks seems to offer an excuse to not take any responsibility. It is much like the blamer approach but instead of blaming someone else or something, the Eeyore approach blames life itself. They make a habit out of being victims to the normal fluctuations of life.

The third approach often taken in response to a fuck up is what I like to call the ricochet approach. This is a radical approach in which, facing failure, one hastily takes their life in the exact opposite way. While this may be merited in certain situations, like when you drank an entire bottle of tequila at the office Christmas party after purchasing the new phone with the upgraded camera. Yes, changing jobs was a must then. However, most challenges in life do not require such extreme measures. Furthermore, constantly using this approach will have you bouncing around, always moving but going nowhere.

Most of us have heard the saying, "get back on the horse." While this may be used to refer to getting a new job or trying again the following week to win the big game, the idiom literally stems from getting bucked off a damn horse. And more importantly, having the tenacity to get back on it again. This is one of the dumbest concepts I can think of. How about getting on a different horse that isn't intent on bucking your ass off? Doesn't that make more sense?

Albert Einstein eloquently explained the fourth way people respond to fucking up. "Insanity," he said, "was doing the same thing over and over again and expecting different results." The man was a literal genius and yet so many people take this very approach. They do the same thing over and over hoping it will somehow generate a different outcome. Their refusal to alter their approach when hitting the brick walls in their lives leaves them nothing but battered and bruise. They never realize taking a different approach to the obstacles may offer a better outcome.

If you want to get anywhere in life, you can't tackle problems by ignoring them or running from them. Problems are not solved by thinking they will go away on their own or blaming them on someone else. The fifth and only approach that results in lasting progress requires a quick refresher of chapter one as you slow the fuck down. Do a mental checklist and evaluate what the hell you know.

"Did I fall down? Yes."

"Is anything broken beyond repair? No."

"Now, what the hell caused me to fall?"

Once we have identified what caused the problem, we can assess ways to go over, around, under, and sometimes, but rarely, through it. When taking a step back, we realize that the problem wasn't the obstacle itself but how we approached it. Sometimes life's most significant challenges lead to the biggest successes. When you stumble, you must take a moment to assess before taking action. You may realize that the exact thing you thought was a stumbling block can be used as a stepping stone instead.

Reflections

Insanity is doing the same
things over and over again and
expecting a different result.

-Albert Einstein

Guidance

Sometimes life's challenges
are tough to deal with. You will
succeed if you focus your thoughts on
how to overcome the challenge.

-Catherine Pulsifer

Advice

No matter what you try to do,
it is better to give your all if you
want any hope of success. Unless you're
giving blood, and that will lead to utter failure.

-One Wise Mother Fucker

Chapter 14
WHEN YOU QUIT, YOU FUCKING FAIL

Life is not always going to be easy. So often, people can't get that simple concept to sink in. Careers, relationships, and life in general take work, and those willing to put in the work are often the most successful. The bar we set on our accomplishments often goes hand in hand with the investment.

Want to make a lot of money? Expect to put in a lot of work. Want that dynamic relationship? You can bet there will be some work involved. Want to get in shape? Again, work, work, and more fucking work. Work doesn't have to be bad, though.

Often, people give up before any reward can be obtained for their efforts. Many people get into the stock market, for example, with dreams of making it rich. Here's looking at you, E*trade, and twenty-year-old me diving in with five hundred bucks I didn't have to spare. I spread my investment between a lumber company, a few penny stocks, and Ford. One month later, I had lost eighty-five dollars and sold all my stock, thankful I didn't squander the rest of my investment cash.

Yes, I was a complete fool because I didn't recognize when you quit, you fucking fail. I am not giving stock or investment advice in any way but the statistics behind quitting and subsequently failing are astonishing. All traders start with big dreams of fast cash and financial freedom. Forty percent lose their nerve within the first month and get out. Eighty percent bail in the first two years. Five years later only seven

126

percent of the people are still wolfing it on Wall Street. Why is this significant?

Take my twenty-year-old dumbass self. I was not a trader and therefore probably wasn't qualified to make stock decisions. Instead of me picking and choosing penny stocks, Ford, and lumber companies, what if I put my money into an index fund and garnered a little patience. For investment noobs like me, an index fund is a collection of stocks that a much smarter person lets you spread your money in. So, for my five hundred dollars, I would own parts of 500 stocks instead of big pieces of a few.

If I had just done that with the five hundred dollars and never touched it again, I would have sixty-eight hundred dollars today. If I continued putting in only an additional five hundred dollars per year, I would now be counting my Sixty-four thousand dollars! No stock market knowledge is required; just don't fucking quit.

Many of us have grown accustomed to simply quitting whenever life gets too hard.

In 2021, Covid caused what has been termed the great resignation, where millions of people left their jobs for various reasons. Some reasons were understandable, such as caring for a loved one or having health and safety concerns. However, a survey conducted by Pew Research looking at the top reasons leaves me scratching my head.

The number one reason why people threw in the towel at work was they felt their pay was too low. Do you know what's worse than a low-paying job? A no-paying job. I've had many low-paying jobs in my life. Some were not enough to even pay the bills. What did I do? I worked to improve my position in my company and my paycheck, or I found another job that paid more. I never quit a stable source of income, no matter how low the pay was, until I had something else lined up.

The second reason given in the survey was that there were no advancement opportunities. The funny thing about opportunities is that they are very rarely given; they are made. Individuals who desire opportunities know they require work, sacrifice, education, and time. Quitting is the exact way to not advance in life. Doing so eliminates all pathways towards the advancement you seek.

Rounding out the top three reasons for quitting was that people felt disrespected in their job. While there is definitely the occasional narcissistic boss who thrives on putting people down, most often, respect is earned. Who is likely gets the most respect? The most capable. Coincidentally, they usually get the most pay and opportunities for advancement as well.

Whenever you feel like you are at the end of your rope and can't do anymore, reflect on those who never quit on you. That parent who worked multiple jobs to put food on the table or the teacher who stayed late to ensure you passed biology. The friend who always listened to your concerns when they would have preferred to be playing Nintendo. When you reflect on the people who never quit on you, it's much easier to find the spark in yourself to keep going. It's not always the fastest or smartest who comes out on top. Often, it's those who don't fucking quit.

Reflections

"Our greatest weakness lies in giving up. The most certain way to succeed is always to try just one more time.

-Thomas Edison

Guidance

"You do what you can for as
long as you can, and when you
finally can't, you do the next best thing.
You back up but you don't give up."

-Chuck Yeager

Advice

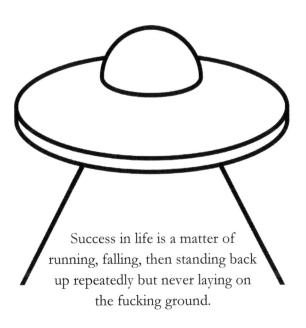

Success in life is a matter of
running, falling, then standing back
up repeatedly but never laying on
the fucking ground.

-One Wise Motherfucker

Chapter 15

WHO YOU ARE SHAPES WHAT YOU FUCKING DO AND WHAT YOU DO SHAPES WHO THE FUCK YOU ARE

When you walk up to someone and ask them who they are, what response do you receive? More often than not, they will tell you what they do. I'm a banker, a teacher, a nurse, a lawyer, etc. Keep the game going, and the responses evolve. They will start to explain they enjoy basketball, listening to music, playing video games, and long walks on the beach. Persist, or allow awkward silence to continue, and new responses include mother, father, brother, sister, etc. will emerge.

There is nothing wrong with these answers, but what was the question? "Who are you?" It is our nature to define who we are by what we do. It's the most natural response because what we choose to do shapes who the fuck we are.

I'm an author. I enjoy writing. I'm creative. I like to share my opinions with others. I enjoy entertaining others.

I'm a teacher. I enjoy helping others. I like helping students develop and learn. I want to be a part of shaping the lives of my students.

What we do shapes who we are. A person who is a doctor has a natural love of science, just like a person that is a lawyer has a passion for law. What you choose to do shapes who you are.

Millions of people will read this book and argue they don't like what they do to make a living; therefore, this point is invalid. I agree every job doesn't necessarily define who a person is. Still, it's what we genuinely choose to do that molds us. What we choose to do isn't the whole story. It's also how we apply ourselves to what we do. Do you work because you want to, or do you work so you can have the money to do other things when the workday is finished? Those other things are what shape you.

Like running marathons? You are shaping your body and mind into a disciplined, powerful tool that can help you in other areas. Like going out with friends to the club? Social development can help you excel in ways that can further your job and relationships.

Likewise, who we are shapes what we do. There are hundreds of surveys that help identify the personality traits that we as individuals have. For example, the Myers Briggs survey identified me as extroverted, intuitive, thinking, and judging. These surveys further suggest different occupations that your personality may be best suited for and even gives you examples of famous people that have shared your "type." Here's looking at you George Clooney. I have taken many of these and love the feedback they provide. They are a starting point for self-reflection but don't concretely define who we are.

We are a highly evolved species that has an innate ability to adapt. While I may be very introverted at work, put me with a group of people I feel comfortable around, and many extroverted qualities spring to life. In my profession, I am a thinker- constantly trying to use logic to solve issues and develop new ideas. Place me with my family, however, and I become more of a feeler than a thinker.

Who we genuinely are at heart can't be captured in a thirty-minute survey, although a good survey can give us glimpses into who we are. The development of who we are comes from a lifetime of experiences. It started at birth and continues throughout our lives.

Ivan Pavlov was a Russian scientist in 1890 who did some unique experiments on his dogs. When placing meat in front of his canines he observed they would salivate in anticipation. Upon further observation, Pavlov observed that the dogs started salivating when the door opened or they heard his footsteps. To test his theory, he began ringing a bell every time he gave his dog meat. After training his dogs this way for weeks, no meat would be required, and the dogs would salivate just at the sound of a bell.

While this experiment is studied in psychology classes all over the world many of us need to recognize that we humans are not Pavlov's dog. Who we are, where we came from, and how we were raised indeed shape who we are, but it doesn't define it. Being born into a poor family doesn't mean that you can't work your ass off, and be the one who pulls your family into a brighter future. Coming from a dysfunctional childhood or even adulthood doesn't mean you don't have a choice of who you allow into your life in the present. You are not Pavlov's dog. While who you are and what you do can be a feedback loop, you can also choose what it loops around. Choose for it to revolve around the best version of you and work to always make it better.

Reflections

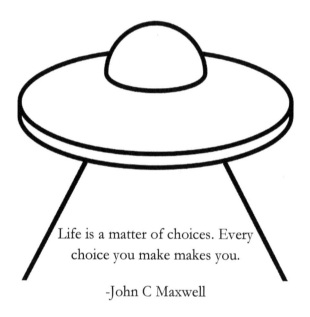

Life is a matter of choices. Every choice you make makes you.

-John C Maxwell

Guidance

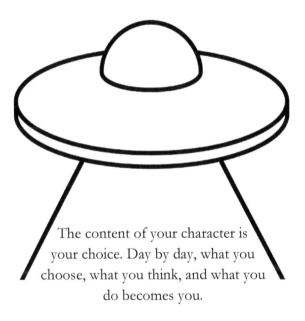

The content of your character is your choice. Day by day, what you choose, what you think, and what you do becomes you.

-Heracles

Advice

Your life is a result of the choices
that you made. If you don't like your
life, it's time to start making better
fucking choices.

-One Wise Mother Fucker

Chapter 16
YOU NEED TO KNOW THE FUCKING DIFFERENCE BETWEEN TAKING CONTROL AND TAKING AWAY

Take fucking control of your life. Pretty damn simple. Countless internet posts, help blogs, therapists, daytime talk show hosts, and even Doc Brown from *Back to the Future* have shared this message repeatedly. It is genuinely good advice. Don't let life dictate who, what, where, or how you will be. Be the controller of your destiny, and don't let anyone or anything stand in your way.

In theory and even practically speaking, there is nothing wrong with this. Taking control imparts within us the ability to overcome obstacles, and triumph over diversity- be the rulers of our own destiny. It imparts a "fuck it" attitude that can push us to greater heights and unshackles us from setbacks. It lets us "get back on the horse," "get our head back in the game," "get back in business, on our feet, and in the ring." Countless colloquialisms define the "fuck it" attitude of taking charge.

Taking control is good, but don't let it lead to a narcissistic outlook that keeps you from seeing how it affects those around you. After all, if you live your life like everything is about you, you will be left with just that. Just you.

In the 1940's severe droughts forced farmers to look for unconventional means to obtain water. With crops drying on the vine before growing to the point of harvest, farmers could do little more than pray as the clouds passed overhead. Daily they begged and pleaded with the sky to release precious rain. In 1946,

American chemist and meteorologist Vincent Schaefer came up with a solution.

Flying over a heavy cloud by plane, he dropped six pounds of crushed dry ice. Almost immediately, snow began to fall. Since then, many different substances have been used to seed clouds, but dry ice remains the most effective. Seeding has been performed using planes, canons, rockets, balloons, and ground generators. For the farmers receiving the rain during a prolonged drought, the efforts are well worth it.

What about the other farmers, though? What about the ones that can't afford planes and rockets to seed the clouds overhead? Is it fair that someone else is retrieving the precious moisture from the sky that may have been destined for their crops?

I'm not bringing up cloud seeding to debate rainstorm politics. I am telling you that you need to be conscious of the people and things around you that need to be watered as well. Many people have had marriages and other relationships come to an end because they were too focused on only seeding the clouds of their careers. Many careers also ended when too much time was spent seeding the clouds of social interaction as opposed to the performance required to succeed in the job at hand.

Taking control of one's life is essential and requires a strong focus on oneself. It requires identifying what to maintain and nourish and what will have to change along the way. We should all look to improve ourselves in all aspects of our lives. Careers, relationships, family, and fortunes can all be enhanced as we focus on the things that need improvement. When doing so, we must avoid getting the kind of neglectful tunnel vision that cuts essential people and ideals from our life.

Most (if not all) people have heard the term "take your blinders off." This term is coined from a piece of equipment used on horses. Blinders on a horse are usually leather flaps extending out to the side of the horse's eyes. With these in place, the horse cannot see behind them and often not even to the sides. This keeps the horse focused on just what is ahead and avoids distractions that may be happening on the periphery.

While we physically place the blinders on horses to increase their efficiency, we often unconsciously put other types of blinders on ourselves. Focus too much on dating the hot chick in your calculus class, and bam… that hot chick became a set of blinders that gave you a D as a final grade. Focus too much on your job to get that promotion and make the big bucks. When you finally get it, you realize that pursuit left you with a ton of money and no family to enjoy it with. Balance, more often than not, beats blinders. The pursuit of greatness is essential to achieve our full potential but do so with the blinders off. This way, when you reach the peak of your mountain, you won't be enjoying the view alone.

Reflections

Once the blinders are off, it's
rather hard to go back to seeing
life the way you used to.

-Mercedes Lackey

Guidance

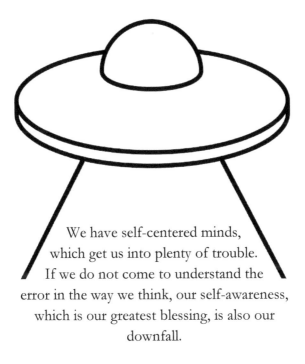

We have self-centered minds,
which get us into plenty of trouble.
If we do not come to understand the
error in the way we think, our self-awareness,
which is our greatest blessing, is also our
downfall.

-Joko Black

Advice

Selfish people really want to keep
or acquire things but, in the process
of doing so, lose as much as they
fucking gain in the process.

-One Wise Mother Fucker

Chapter 17

WHAT IS YOUR FUCKING FUEL

What is the motivating factor that enables you to move forward toward your goals? What allows you to keep pushing when others give up long before the finish line? Essentially, what fuels your grit? Identifying what motivates you can be a catalyst to greatness, or at least to taking your first steps towards greatness. At its core, motivation is the force that drives you to perform a task or behavior. While our motivating factors can come in many different forms, the primary purpose is to ignite a spark within us for our own productivity.

Fire is fire. Crumble up some papers, and they burn with the light of a match. Build your campfire with twigs and sticks, and with the strike of a flint, fire is made. Nomads who couldn't find wood to start their fires burned the dried-up shit from their livestock. Yes, even shit can be your fucking fuel source. This is important to remember when we dig deeper into the different types of motivation.

First, we have intrinsic motivation. Intrinsic motivation is all the internal things that push us to be whatever the fuck we are to be. The desire to learn, our overall attitude, our sense of achievement, and the desire to create all fall into this category. It's the reason I have a Spotify playlist titled, "Fuck it!" It's filled with all the songs that pit me against the world. It's also why I have a "Good Vibes" playlist for other days and another titled "Chill" Because you know, sometimes you gotta chill.

The intrinsic factors are often harder to pull from, but these types of motivation have the longest-lasting effects. After all, they are ours and generally free of outside influence. They are the factors that often drive the Steve Jobs and Elon Musks of the world. Yes, the billion dollars in the bank account is nice, but the money is not what pushes great minds forward.

There are three ways you can increase your intrinsic motivation. First, you have to establish an understanding of your own autonomy. Your decisions and actions are the primary factors in your success. It is easy for us to get caught up in a viewpoint that our place in life is due to various outside causes (the victim mentality). We look at those who have found success and try to rationalize that they got lucky or that we haven't gotten our big break. The first step in finding intrinsic motivation is realizing that, ultimately, you are responsible for you.

Second, we must understand how our actions relate to our future success. Want to be in great shape? You need to know how the action of working out and having a good diet relates to your physical fitness- especially over time. Want to be a writer? You better understand how words require reflection and effort, then put that shit down on paper. Want to be an "influencer?" You better know what other people want, how to build great content, and how to use the platforms that will bring it to your audience. Personally, I believe everyone is an influencer. It's just that some people happen to have far larger audiences to influence.

Lastly, our own competence drives our intrinsic motivation. Go back fifty years, and this was a much more detrimental factor. Today, a lack of competence is often attributed to laziness. Don't know how to work out and eat right? Google that shit. Don't know how to use Microsoft Word for the job you want? YouTube that shit. Gone are the days of flipping through the Encyclopedia Brittanica or spending hours in the library to understand the migratory patterns of South American bat populations. Knowledge is everywhere! The quicker we take control of our own learning and development, the faster we can find and grow our internal motivation.

Extrinsic motivating factors are much easier to recognize and respond to. They are most often a product of our environment or our desire to fit into it in a certain way. Scared of having a medical issue because you just found out a guy you graduated with had a heart attack? Say hello to the extrinsic factor of fear. Want to lose some weight and get in shape in hopes of getting that particular person's eye and punching your one-way ticket to shag town? Sex may be your external incentive.

External factors come in many forms, from the desire for power, social acceptance, or any other primal urges the human species tends to have. They are quick, and easy to recognize but not nearly as long-lasting as the intrinsic ones. That doesn't mean they are without merit.

Often our extrinsic motivator can be the initial fuel that builds into intrinsic ones. You may be brushing up on your Spanish to speak with a new colleague at work but find that learning a new language opens up other doors and opportunities for advancement. Maybe you start working out because you don't want to end up with the heart attack your classmate had. Then you realize you feel better, have more energy, and get through the days more effortlessly now that you are in better shape.

Whether it's an internal drive or outside factors squeezing you, remember that anything can be your fuel. It doesn't matter if what motivates you isn't the typical thing others would use to drive them forward. Your fire can be completely unique to you. What matters is that you light that shit on fire and get going. With every step, you improve yourself; come hell or high water. Never fear the failures of tomorrow. Be fearful that you might wake up in the same place as you are today.

Reflections

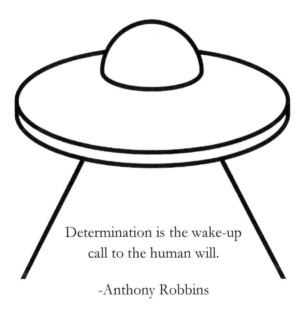

Determination is the wake-up
call to the human will.

-Anthony Robbins

Guidance

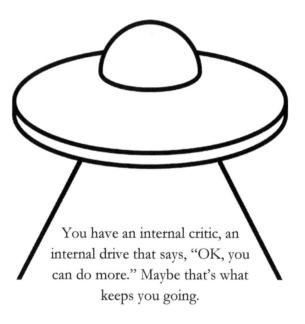

You have an internal critic, an
internal drive that says, "OK, you
can do more." Maybe that's what
keeps you going.

-Robin Williams

Advice

The greatest fucking oak tree
was once a little nut who held his
ground and kept growing.

-One Wise Mother Fucker

Chapter 18
SOMETIMES IT'S SIMPLY ABOUT YOUR FUCKING PERSPECTIVE

John Godrey Saxe was an American poet who lived from 1716 to 1769. His most famous poem was a retelling of the Indian parable of *The Blind Men and the Elephant.* In this poem he eloquently expressed how six blind men understood an elephant standing before them. Like Saxe did 300 years ago, I shall share this poem of infinite wisdom from my perspective.

> There were six dudes from Dallas,
> Who all desired to find,
> The makings of an elephant,
> Though all of them were blind,

The first approached so cautiously,
But happened to trip and fall,
Against this mighty side of the beast,
And he began to yelp and call,
Holy shit motherfuckers,
It's nothing but a wall!

The second reached out and grabbed a tusk,
Well damn, what have we here,
It's round and smooth and very sharp,
It seems pretty fucking clear,
This thing they call an elephant,
Is really a fucking spear!

The third approached the animal,
And he just happened to take,
A squirming trunk within his hands,
Oh shit, it is a snake!

The fourth reached out with an eager hand,
and rubbed against its knee,
You other dumb motherfuckers need to
wake the hell up,
It's obviously a tree!

The fifth just happened to touch its ear
and said even the blindest man,
Can tell what an elephant is mostly like;
it's mostly like a fan!

The sixth dude had just begun,
upon the beast, he groped,
When between its butt cheeks, he grabbed
the tale that fell within his scope,
I see exactly what we have here;
it's like a fucking rope!

And so, these guys argued loud and long,
their opinions were firm and strong,
Though each of them was partly right
they all were really wrong!

Sometimes in life, it is necessary to get a different viewpoint. Often, when we think everything is perfect, it is quite the opposite. Likewise, sometimes when we feel the sky is falling, things are much better than they may seem on the surface.

I was talking to my son when I referenced how things were better now. I spoke of how crazy and hard it was when we were poor. "Wait a sec," he replied. "We were poor?"

I reminded him of the 100-degree summers in a car with no air conditioning, and with windows that didn't roll down.

"But we were always taking it to the movies," he replied.

I explained that the movie theatre we went to was a dollar theatre, and that's why we went to it.

"I just thought it was because that theatre had the best popcorn," he countered.

Same car, same movie, same financial situation but an entirely different perspective.

I also remember vividly the phone call I got at work from my dad when I was twenty-two. My dad never called my work, so I feared the worst. After answering and some brief small talk, he informed me that 98% of his prostate was cancer-free. "You have prostate cancer?" I asked after an awkward silence.

"No," he quickly corrected. "98% of my prostate is cancer free and we will get the remaining 2% in line." After a little over a year, a few rounds of radiation, and a positive attitude he remains cancer free to this day. Perspective!

We need to be constantly gathering different perspectives. The easiest way to do this is to ask the opinion of people you can trust to speak honestly. This doesn't mean finding people to say what you want to hear.

When I wrote my first book, I thought it would be brilliant to have my mother proofread it. After all, she was an English major and had taught literature for a long time. I waited over a week for her markup of my manuscript. When I finally got it, I was floored by how many marks were made on each page. The manuscript was thoroughly rifled with grammatical errors, but her markings never pointed them out. Page after page of "I really like this," "great job," and "I'm very proud," etc. was the only feedback. What was that feedback worth to me? Absolute shit like the quality of the writing.

When choosing people to give you new perspectives, you must choose wisely. Choosing someone that doesn't want to hurt your feelings or offend you in any way only gives you feedback that, at best, is partially true. You need to be able to hear the good and the bad. Sometimes, the best people to listen to are actually your enemies.

I'm not implying that you pick fights with people just to gain a little perspective. However, the people that you sometimes butt heads with can give you insights you may not receive anywhere else. The people most critical of you often have some grain of truth to what they are saying. It may be exaggerated and petty, but it gives us a different perspective.

This doesn't mean you have to internalize criticism and take everyone else's opinion to heart. It does mean you walk through life realizing that other perspectives can be important. In doing so, you allow yourself to expand, reflect, and grow as a human being. Considering new perspectives isn't always easy. Sometimes it can even be humbling, but only through expanded perspective can we realize our full potential.

Reflections

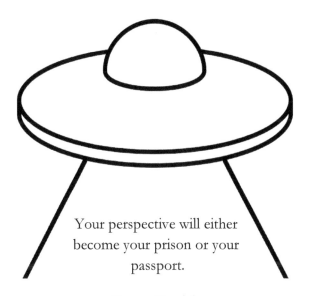

Your perspective will either
become your prison or your
passport.

Steven Furtick

Guidance

If you don't like something,
Change it. If you can't change it,
change the way you think about it.

Mary Engelbreit

Advice

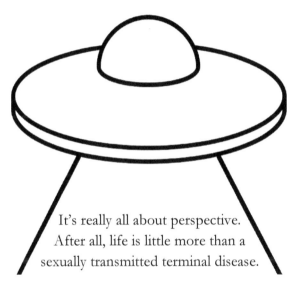

It's really all about perspective.
After all, life is little more than a
sexually transmitted terminal disease.

-One Wise Mother Fucker

Chapter 19

THE MORE YOU FUCKING ARE, THE LESS YOU FUCKING NEED.

The world we live in focuses so much attention on the material possessions we own. Many hard-working people struggle to make a decent living wage, much less an ability to thrive in society. The desire to be seen as having your life together goes beyond socioeconomic boundaries. Drive through any town, and it's easy to see. Houses with paint peeling and leaky roofs worth no more than $60k will have $80k cars parked in their driveways. Why would the owners not purchase a more reasonably priced vehicle and fix up their homes? Because it's the car that they take to work, the grocery store, and the club where they get seen. Being seen in fancy vehicles for some, makes them feel like they are something fancy themselves.

Looking at the truly successful people of the world, you see a different hierarchy of values. Einstein had several sets of the same outfit he wore day after day. He believed his mind should be focused on more important things other than picking out his daily attire. Steve Jobs was very similar with the turtlenecks, jeans, and gym shoes he frequently wore. Keanu Reeves, the fifth highest-grossing actor of all time, can routinely be seen riding the subway. These are examples of people who knew exactly who they were and found value in what they were far more than what they had. Highly successful and productive people organize their lives in such ways to eliminate wasted time, effort, and even thoughts.

It's not just high performing experts, gurus, or industry titans who understand the power of simplicity by elimination. What would you guess is the number one vehicle driven by millionaires? Maserati's screaming down the autobahn? Fully loaded Teslas with the autopilot feature already engaged? The most commonly driven vehicle by the world's millionaires is the Ford F-150 pickup truck. Simple, rugged, and the number one choice of millionaires. Could they be driving around in something much more exotic and high-end? Sure. Do they feel the need to? Hell no!

You don't have to be a millionaire but when you truly appreciate who you have become, what you have has far less meaning. You don't need likes on social media or big jealous eyeballs staring at your car or what you wear: you are a badass and you know it. You care far less about what others think of you because you know yourself better than anyone possibly could.

This doesn't mean you aren't assessed, evaluated, or graded. It means that you develop the rubric and assign the grade accordingly. When you grade yourself lower than your expectations, it's you that develops the remediation plan for your life to score higher next time.

There are no bonus points for fancy cars, houses, boats, or elaborate social media accounts. You are the one person that always has an inside view of what really makes you, you. So many people hide behind the things they have because they can't accept who they are. They see the super successful and assume their lives have no problems. It really does appear that most super celebrities' lives are perfect. That is by design.

There are several very universal things everyone deals with. No matter your wealth, position, or status, we all share these things. First, we all have had, currently have, or will have some emotional pain. Be it from insecurity, fear, self-doubt, a sense of not belonging, or personal trauma, it's something everyone deals with at some point.

Second, self-confidence is a learned behavior. No one is born with it. Hell, some people who appear to have it are simply faking it until they feel it. Learning self-confidence will stretch your comfort levels as you put yourself in new and uncomfortable situations. With practice, anyone can gain this skill.

Third, the loudest and most insidious voice you will ever hear will come from within yourself. It will often tell you that you must be perfect in all things. It tells you every mistake you make is the end of the world when really, it's an opportunity to learn and do better next time. We must hear our inner voice but also temper it when need be.

Lastly, you don't need to know what everyone thinks. This is a trap we all continually fall into. You can't control what others think, but you can take ownership of who you are. This is ultimately what the really successful people figure out. Your relationship with yourself determines your relationship with everything else. When you learn who you are, the "whats" in life don't matter nearly as much.

Reflection

Be yourself. Everyone else
is already taken.

-Oscar Wilde

Guidance

To be yourself in a world that is constantly trying to make you something else is the greatest accomplishment.

-Ralph Waldo Emerson

Advice

Always be yourself. Unless
you can be Dwayne Johnson
then be the fucking Rock.

One Wise Motherfucker

Chapter 20

FINAL FUCKING THOUGHTS

The one certainty about life is that it will be uncertain. The struggles and obstacles that each of us face will be completely unique. While this guarantees there is no general recipe for success applying to everyone, it also ensures that there is an endless growing and evolving repertoire of fuck ups we can all learn from.

When writing this book, I often found myself looking to the past. Pondering my childhood, adolescence, and even adulthood, I discovered some of the most valuable tidbits of knowledge I acquired through my mistakes.

It is easy to look upon our setbacks and regard them as something that puts us down. After all, that is what most of the world tends to do for us. When you learn something from them, you empower yourself going forward.

What do you get out of a sponge whenever you squeeze it? Whatever the hell it soaked up. In the good and the bad, the triumph or the failure, make sure you are absorbing something to help you going forward. Every situation is an opportunity to learn. Life isn't going to be easy, and it isn't going to be fair, so when the pressures of life squeeze you, make sure your sponge is ready.

Obstacles and even failures are a requirement for success. After all, a sponge is most effective when it is damp. Always look to soak up the lessons of life. Along the way, write into your life and those around you your own personal book of simple advice.

Thank you for taking the time to read through the words of wisdom offered in these simple pages. Please feel free to reach out to me with your own words of simple advice at:

simeone@simpleadviceforhumans.com

Also, if you would like to leave a book review for this simple advice, it can be done so at the following:

http://www.amazon.com/review/create-review?&asin=B0CWYD247C

Milton Keynes UK
Ingram Content Group UK Ltd.
UKHW022218130524
442669UK00006B/103

9 780983 654223